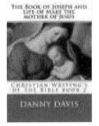

The History of Joseph the Carpenter & Mary the Mother of Jesus

Copyright © 2010 by Danny Davis
All rights fully reserved,
All World rights reserved.
reno_27320@yahoo.com

ISBN   1-441-429042
ISBN   13: 978-1-441-429049.

Introduction

This book is based on fore ancient Writings, The Holy Bible, and the book of Joseph the carpenter and the book of Mary the mother of Jesus by James the less. The Death of Mary the mother of Jesus. The last three books are part of the Christian writing collection. Studying this collection of books helps us better understand the Bible and the times of that day. One thing to remember when reading the Christian writing collection is there was no church denominations back in this time in History, denominations came with men's disagreeing over doctrine and church authority.

Comparing the last three books we find the answer to seven common questions ask today.

1. How old was Mary when Jesus was conceived?
2. How old was Jesus when Joseph Died?
3. Did Jesus have any brother and sisters?
4. Who were the parents of Mary?
5. How did Mary and Joseph meet

6. How old was Joseph when Jesus was born

7. Why was John the Baptist, not killed by Herod the great?

Introduction to the History of Josephs the carpenter

His whole life was one hundred and eleven years, and his departure from this world happened on the twenty-sixth of the month Abib, which answers to the month Ab. May his prayer preserve us! Amen. And, indeed, it was our Lord Jesus Christ Himself who related this history to His holy disciples on the Mount of Olives, and all Joseph's labour, and the end of his days. And the holy apostles have preserved this conversation, and have left it written down in the library at Jerusalem. May their prayers preserve us! Amen.

History of Josephs the carpenter

1. It happened one day, when the Saviour, our Master, God, and Saviour Jesus Christ, was sitting along with His disciples, and they were all assembled on the Mount of Olives, that He said to them: O my brethren and friends, sons of the Father who has chosen you from all men, you know that I have often told you that I must be crucified,

and must die for the salvation of Adam and his posterity, and that I shall rise from the dead. Now I shall commit to you the doctrine of the holy gospel formerly announced to you, that you may declare it. Throughout the whole world. And I shall endow you with power from on high, and fill you with the Holy Spirit. And you shall declare to all nations' repentance and remission of sins. For a single cup of water, if a man shall find it in the world to come, is greater and better than all the wealth of this whole world. And as much ground as one foot can occupy in the house of my Father, is greater and more excellent than all the riches of the earth. Yea, a single hour in the joyful dwelling of the pious is more blessed and more precious than a thousand years among sinners: inasmuch as their weeping and lamentation shall not come to an end, and their tears shall not cease, nor shall they find for themselves consolation and repose at any time for ever. And now, O my honored members, go declare to all nations, tell them, and say to them: Verily the Saviour diligently inquires into the inheritance which is due, and is the administrator of justice. And the angels will cast down their enemies, and will fight for them in the day of conflict. And He will examine every single foolish and idle word which men speak, and they shall give an account of it. For as no one shall escape death, so also the works of every man shall be laid open on the day of judgment, whether they have been good or evil. Tell them also this word which I have said to you to-day: Let not the strong man glory in his strength, nor the rich man in his riches; but let him who wishes to glory, glory in the Lord.

2. There was a man whose name was Joseph, sprung from a family of Bethlehem, a town of Judah, and the city of King David. This same man, being well furnished with wisdom and learning, was made a priest in the temple of the Lord. He was, besides. skilful in his trade, which was that of a carpenter; and after the manner of all men, he married a wife. Moreover, he begot for himself sons and daughters, four sons, namely, and two daughters. Now these are their names--Judas, Justus, James, and Simon. The names of the two daughters were Assia and Lydia. At length the wife of righteous Joseph, a woman intent on the divine glory in all her works, departed this life. But Joseph, that righteous man, my father after the flesh, and the spouse of my mother Mary, went away with his sons to his trade, practicing the art of a carpenter.

3. Now when righteous Joseph became a widower, my mother Mary, blessed, holy, and pure, was already twelve years old. For her parents offered her in the temple when she was three years of age, and she remained in the temple of the Lord nine years. Then when the priests saw that the virgin, holy and God-fearing, was growing up, they spoke to each other, saying: Let us search out a man, righteous and pious, to whom Mary may be entrusted until the time of her marriage; lest, if she remain in the temple, it happen to her as is wont to happen to women, and lest on that account we sin, and God be angry with us.

4. Therefore they immediately sent out, and assembled twelve old men of the tribe of Judah. And they wrote down the names of the twelve tribes of Israel. And the lot fell upon the pious old man, righteous Joseph. Then the priests answered, and said to my blessed mother: Go with Joseph, and be with him till the time of your marriage. Righteous Joseph therefore received my mother, and led her away to his own house. And Mary found James the Less in his father's house, broken-hearted and sad on account of the loss of his mother, and she brought him up. Hence Mary was called the mother of James. Thereafter Joseph left her at home, and went away to the shop where he wrought at his

trade of a carpenter. And after the holy virgin had spent two years in his house her age was exactly fourteen years, including the time at which he received her.

5. And I chose her of my own will, with the concurrence of my Father, and the counsel of the Holy Spirit. And I was made flesh of her, by a mystery which transcends the grasp of created reason. And three months after her conception the righteous man Joseph returned from the place where he worked at his trade; and when he found my virgin mother pregnant, he was greatly perplexed, and thought of sending her away secretly. But from fear, and sorrow, and the anguish of his heart, he could endure neither to eat nor drink that day.

6. But at mid-day there appeared to him in a dream the prince of the angels, the holy Gabriel, furnished with a command from my Father; and he said to him: Joseph, son of David, fear not to take Mary as thy wife: for she has conceived of the Holy Spirit; and she will bring forth a son, whose name shall be called Jesus. He it is who shall rule all nations with a rod of iron. Having thus spoken, the angel departed from him. And Joseph rose from his sleep, and did as the angel of the Lord had said to him; and Mary abode with him.

7. Some time after that, there came forth an order from Augustus Caesar the king, that all the habitable world should be enrolled, each man in his own city. The old man therefore, righteous Joseph, rose up and took the virgin Mary and came to Bethlehem, because the time of her bringing forth was at hand. Joseph then inscribed his name in the list; for Joseph the son of David, whose spouse Mary was, was of the tribe of Judah. And indeed Mary, my mother, brought me forth in Bethlehem, in a cave near the tomb of Rachel the wife of the patriarch Jacob, the mother of Joseph and Benjamin.

8. But Satan went and told this to Herod the Great, the father of Archelaus. And it was this same Herod who ordered my friend and relative John to be beheaded. Accordingly he searched for me diligently, thinking that my kingdom was to be of this world. But Joseph, that pious old man, was warned of this by a dream. Therefore he rose and took Mary my mother, and I lay in her bosom. Salome also was their fellow-traveller. Having therefore set out from home, he retired into Egypt, and remained there the space of one whole year, until the hatred of Herod passed away.

9. Now Herod died by the worst form of death, atoning for the shedding of the blood of the children whom he wickedly cut off,

though there was no sin in them. And that impious tyrant Herod being dead, they returned into the land of Israel, and lived in a city of Galilee which is called Nazareth. And Joseph, going back to his trade of a carpenter, earned his living by the work of his hands; for, as the law of Moses had commanded, he never sought to live for nothing by another's labor.

10. At length, by increasing years, the old man arrived at a very advanced age. He did not, however, labor under any bodily weakness, nor had his sight failed, nor had any tooth perished from his mouth. In mind also, for the whole time of his life, he never wandered; but like a boy he always in his business displayed youthful vigour, and his limbs remained unimpaired, and free from all pain. His life, then, in all, amounted to one hundred and eleven years, his old age being prolonged to the utmost limit.

11. Now Justus and Simeon, the eider sons of Joseph, were married, and had families of their own. Both the daughters were likewise married, and lived in their own houses. So there remained in Joseph's house, Judas and James the Less, and my virgin mother. I moreover dwelt along with them, not otherwise than if I had been one of his sons. But I passed all my life without fault. Mary I called my mother, and Joseph father, and I

obeyed them in all that they said; nor did I ever contend against them, but complied with their commands, as other men whom earth produces are wont to do; nor did I at any time arouse their anger, or give any word or answer in opposition to them. On the contrary, I cherished them with great love, like the pupil of my eye.

12. It came to pass, after these things that the death of that old man, the pious Joseph, and his departure from this world, were approaching, as happens to other men who owe their origin to this earth. And as his body was verging on dissolution, an angel of the Lord informed him that his death was now close at hand. Therefore fear and great perplexity came upon him. So he rose up and went to Jerusalem; and going into the temple of the Lord, he poured out his prayers there before the sanctuary, and said:

13. O God! author of all consolation, God of all compassion, and Lord of the whole human race; God of my soul, body, and spirit; with supplications I reverence thee, O Lord and my God. If now my days are ended, and the time draws near when I must leave this world, send me, I beseech Thee, the great Michael, the prince of Thy holy angels: let him remain with me, that my wretched soul may depart from this afflicted body without trouble, without terror and

impatience. For great fear and intense sadness take hold of all bodies on the day of their death, whether it be man or woman, beast wild or tame, or whatever creeps on the ground or flies in the air. At the last all creatures under heaven in whom is the breath of life are struck with horror, and their souls depart from their bodies with strong fear and great depression. Now therefore, O Lord and my God let Thy holy angel be present with his help to my soul and body, until they shall be dissevered from each other. And let not the face of the angel, appointed my guardian from the day of my birth, be turned away from me; but may he be the companion of my journey even until he bring me to Thee: let his countenance be pleasant and gladsome to me, and let him accompany me in peace. And let not demons of frightful aspect come near me in the way in which I am to go, until I come to Thee in bliss. And let not the doorkeepers hinder my soul from entering paradise. And do not uncover my sins, and expose me to condemnation before Thy terrible tribunal. Let not the lions rush in upon me; nor let the waves of the sea of fire overwhelm my soul--for this must every soul pass through -- before I have seen the glory of Thy Godhead. O God, most righteous Judge, who in justice and equity wilt judge

mankind, and wilt render unto each one
according to his works, O Lord and my God,
I beseech Thee, be present to me in Thy
compassion, and enlighten my path that I
may come to Thee; for Thou art a fountain
overflowing with all good things, and with
glory for evermore. Amen.

14. It came to pass thereafter, when he
returned to his own house in the city of
Nazareth, that he was seized by disease, and
had to keep his bed. And it was at this time
that he died, according to the destiny of all
mankind. For this disease was very heavy
upon him, and he had never been ill, as he
now was, from the day of his birth. And thus
assuredly it pleased Christ to order the
destiny of righteous Joseph. He lived forty
years unmarried; thereafter his wife
remained under his care forty-nine years,
and then died. And a year after her death,
my mother, the blessed Mary, was entrusted
to him by the priests, that he should keep her
until the time of her marriage. She spent two
years in his house; and in the third year of
her stay with Joseph, in the fifteenth year of
her age, she brought me forth on earth by a
mystery which no creature can penetrate or
understand, except myself, and my Father
and the Holy Spirit, constituting one essence
with myself.

15. The whole age of my father, therefore, that righteous old man, was one hundred and eleven years, my Father in heaven having so decreed. And the day on which his soul left his body was the twenty-sixth of the month Abib. For now the fine gold began to lose its splendour, and the silver to be worn down by use--I mean his understanding and his wisdom. He also loathed food and drink, and lost all his skill in his trade of carpentry, nor did he any more pay attention to it. It came to pass, then, in the early dawn of the twenty-sixth day of Abib that Joseph, that righteous old man, lying in his bed, was giving up his unquiet soul. Wherefore he opened his mouth with many sighs, and struck his hands one against the other, and with a loud voice cried out, and spoke after the following manner:--

16. Woe to the day on which I was born into the world! Woe to the womb which bare me! Woe to the bowels which admitted me! Woe to the breasts which suckled me! Woe to the feet upon which I sat and rested! Woe to the hands which carried me and reared me until I grew up! For I was conceived in iniquity, and in sins did my mother desire me. Woe to my tongue and my lips, which have brought forth and spoken vanity, detraction, falsehood, ignorance, derision, idle tales, craft, and hypocrisy! Woe to mine eyes,

which have looked upon scandalous things! Woe to mine ears, which have delighted in the words of slanderers! Woe to my hands, which have seized what did not of right belong to them! Woe to my belly and my bowels, which have lusted after food unlawful to be eaten! Woe to my throat, which like a fire has consumed all that it found! Woe to my feet, which have too often walked in ways displeasing to God! Woe to my body; and woe to my miserable soul, which has already turned aside from God its Maker! What shall I do when I arrive at that place where I must stand before the most righteous Judge, and when He shall call me to account for the works which I have heaped up in my youth? Woe to every man dying in his sins! Assuredly that same dreadful hour, which came upon my father Jacob, when his soul was flying forth from his body, is now, behold, near at hand for me. Oh! how wretched I am this day, and worthy of lamentation! But God alone is the disposer of my soul and body; He also will deal with them after His own good pleasure.

17. These are the words spoken by Joseph, that righteous old man. And I, going in beside him, found his soul exceedingly troubled, for he was placed in great perplexity. And I said to him: Hail! My

father Joseph, thou righteous man; how is it with thee? And he answered me: All hail! My well-beloved son. Indeed, the agony and fear of death have already environed me; but as soon as I heard Thy voice, my soul was at rest. O Jesus of Nazareth! Jesus, my Savior! Jesus, the deliverer of my soul! Jesus, my protector! Jesus! O sweetest name in my mouth, and in the mouth of all those that love it! O eye which seest, and ear which hearest, hear me! I am Thy servant; this day I most humbly reverence Thee, and before Thy face I pour out my tears. Thou art altogether my God; Thou art my Lord, as the angel has told me times without number, and especially on that day when my soul was driven about with perverse thoughts about the pure and blessed Mary, who was carrying Thee in her womb, and whom I was thinking of secretly sending away. And while I was thus meditating, behold, there appeared to me in my rest angels of the Lord, saying to me in a wonderful mystery: O Joseph, thou son of David, fear not to take Mary as thy wife; and do not grieve thy soul, nor speak unbecoming words of her conception, because she is with child of the Holy Spirit, and shall bring forth a son, whose name shall be called Jesus, for He shall save His people from their sins. Do not for this cause wish me evil, O Lord! for I was ignorant of the mystery of Thy birth. I call to mind also, my Lord, that day when the boy died of the bite of the serpent. And his relations wished to deliver Thee to Herod, saying that Thou hadst killed him; but Thou didst raise him from the dead, and restore him to them. Then I went up to Thee, and took hold of Thy hand, saying: My son, take care of thyself. But Thou didst say to me in reply: Art thou not my father after the flesh? I shall teach thee who I am. Now therefore, O Lord and my God, do not be angry with me, or condemn me on account of that hour. I am Thy servant, and the son of Thine handmaiden; but Thou art my Lord, my God and Savior, most surely the Son of God.

18. When my father Joseph had thus spoken, he was unable to weep more. And I saw that death now had dominion over him. And my mother, virgin undefiled, rose and came to me, saying: O my beloved son, this pious old man Joseph is now dying. And I answered: Oh my dearest mother, assuredly upon all creatures produced in this world the same necessity of death lies; for death holds sway over the whole human race. Even thou, O my virgin mother, must look for the same end of life as other mortals. And yet thy death, as also the death of this pious man, is not death, but life enduring to eternity. Nay

more, even I must die, as concerns the body which I have received from thee. But rise, O my venerable mother, and go in to Joseph, that blessed old man, in order that thou mayst see what will happen as his soul ascends from his body.

19. My undefiled mother Mary, therefore, went and entered the place where Joseph was. And I was sitting at his feet looking at him, for the signs of death already appeared in his countenance. And that blessed old man raised his head, and kept his eyes fixed on my face; but he had no power of speaking to me, on account of the agonies of death, which held him in their grasp. But he kept fetching many sighs. And I held his hands for a whole hour; and he turned his face to me, and made signs for me not to leave him. Thereafter I put my hand upon his breast, and perceived his soul now near his throat, preparing to depart from its receptacle.

20. And when my virgin mother saw me touching his body, she also touched his feet. And finding them already dead and destitute of heat, she said to me: O my beloved son, assuredly his feet are already beginning to stiffen, and they are as cold as snow. Accordingly she summoned his sons and daughters, and said to them: Come, as many as there are of you, and go to your father; for

assuredly he is now at the very point of death. And Assia, his daughter, answered and said: Woe's me, O my brothers, this is certainly the same disease that my beloved mother died of. And she lamented and shed tears; and all Joseph's other children mourned along with her. I also, and my mother Mary, wept along with them.

21. And turning my eyes towards the region of the south, I saw Death already approaching, and all Gehenna with him, closely attended by his army and his satellites; and their clothes, their faces, and their mouths poured forth flames. And when my father Joseph saw them coming straight to him, his eyes dissolved in tears, and at the same time he groaned after a strange manner. Accordingly, when I saw the vehemence of his sighs, I drove back Death and all the host of servants which accompanied him. And I called upon my good Father, saying:--

22. O Father of all mercy, eye which seest, and ear which hearest, hearken to my prayers and supplications in behalf of the old man Joseph; and send Michael, the prince of Thine angels, and Gabriel, the herald of light, and all the light of Thine angels, and let their whole array walk with the soul of my father Joseph, until they shall have conducted it to Thee. This is the hour

in which my father has need of compassion. And I say unto you, that all the saints, yea, as many men as are born in the world, whether they be just or whether they be perverse, must of necessity taste of death. 23. Therefore Michael and Gabriel came to the soul of my father Joseph, and took it, and wrapped it in a shining wrapper. Thus he committed his spirit into the hands of my good Father, and He bestowed upon him peace. But as yet none of his children knew that he had fallen asleep. And the angels preserved his soul from the demons of darkness which were in the way, and praised God even until they conducted it into the dwelling-place of the pious.

24. Now his body was lying prostrate and bloodless; wherefore I reached forth my hand, and put right his eyes and shut his mouth, and said to the virgin Mary: O my mother, where is the skill which he showed in all the time that he lived in this world? Lo! it has perished, as if it had never existed. And when his children heard me speaking with my mother, the pure virgin, they knew that he had already breathed his last, and they shed tears, and lamented. But I said to them: Assuredly the death of your father is not death, but life everlasting: for he has been freed from the troubles of this life, and has passed to perpetual and everlasting rest.

When they heard these words, they rent their clothes, and wept.

25. And, indeed, the inhabitants of Nazareth and of Galilee, having heard of their lamentation, flocked to them, and wept from the third hour even to the ninth. And at the ninth hour they all went together to Joseph's bed. And they lifted his body, after they had anointed it with costly unguents. But I entreated my Father in the prayer of the celestials--that same prayer which with any own hand I made before I was carried in the womb of the virgin Mary, my mother. And as soon as I had finished it, and pronounced the amen, a great multitude of angels came up; and I ordered two of them to stretch out their shining garments, and to wrap in them the body of Joseph, the blessed old man.

26. And I spoke to Joseph, and said: The smell or corruption of death shall not have dominion over thee, nor shall a worm ever come forth from thy body. Not a single limb of it shall be broken, nor shall any hair on thy head be changed. Nothing of thy body shall perish, O my father Joseph, but it will remain entire and uncorrupted even until the banquet of the thousand years. And whosoever shall make an offering on the day of thy remembrance, him will I bless and recompense in the congregation of the virgins; and whosoever shall give food to

the wretched, the poor, the widows, and orphans from the work of his hands, on the day on which thy memory shall be celebrated, and in thy name, shall not be in want of good things all the days of his life. And whosoever shall have given a cup of water, or of wine, to drink to the widow or orphan in thy name, I will give him to thee, that thou mayst go in with him to the banquet of the thousand years. And every man who shall present an offering on the day of thy commemoration will I bless and recompense in the church of the virgins: for one I will render unto him thirty, sixty, and a hundred. And whosover shall write the history of thy life, of thy labour, and thy departure from this world, and this narrative that has issued from my mouth, him shall I commit to thy keeping as long as he shall have to do with this life. And when his soul departs from the body, and when he must leave this world, I will bum the book of his sins, nor will I torment him with any punishment in the day of judgment; but he shall cross the sea of flames, and shall go through it without trouble or pain. And upon every poor man who can give none of those things which I have mentioned this is incumbent: viz., if a son is born to him, he shall call his name Joseph. So there shall not take place in that house either poverty or any sudden death for ever.

27. Thereafter the chief men of the city came together to the place where the body of the blessed old man Joseph had been laid, bringing with them burial-clothes; and they wished to wrap it up in them after the manner in which the Jews are wont to arrange their dead bodies. And they perceived that he kept his shroud fast; for it adhered to the body in such a way, that when they wished to take it off, it was found to be like iron--impossible to be moved or loosened. Nor could they find any ends in that piece of linen, which struck them with the greatest astonishment. At length they carried him out to a place where there was a cave, and opened the gate, that they might bury his body beside the bodies of his fathers. Then there came into my mind the day on which he walked with me into Egypt, and that extreme trouble which he endured on my account. Accordingly, I bewailed his death for a long time; and lying upon his body, I said:--

28. O Death! who makest all knowledge to vanish away, and raisest so many tears and lamentations, surely it is God my Father Himself who hath granted thee this power. For men die for the transgression of Adam and his wife Eve, and Death spares not so

much as one. Nevertheless, nothing happens to any one, or is brought upon him, without the command of my Father. There have certainly been men who have prolonged their life even to nine hundred years; but they died. Yea, though some of them have lived longer, they have, notwithstanding, succumbed to the same fate; nor has any one of them ever said: I have not tasted death. For the Lord never sends the same punishment more than once, since it hath pleased my Father to bring it upon men. And at the very moment when it, going forth, beholds the command descending to it from heaven, it says: I will go forth against that man, and will greatly move him. Then, without delay, it makes an onset on the soul, and obtains the mastery of it, doing with it whatever it will. For, because Adam did not the will of my Father, but transgressed His commandment, the wrath of my Father was kindled against him, and He doomed him to death; and thus it was that death came into the world. But if Adam had observed my Father's precepts, death would never have fallen to his lot. Think you that I can ask my good Father to send me a chariot of fire, which may take up the body of my father Joseph, and convey it to the place of rest, in order that it may dwell with the spirits? But on account of the transgression of Adam, that trouble and violence of death has descended upon all the human race. And it is for this cause that I must die according to the flesh, for my work which I have created, that they may obtain grace.

29. Having thus spoken, I embraced the body of my father Joseph, and wept over it; and they opened the door of the tomb, and placed his body in it, near the body of his father Jacob. And at the time when he fell asleep he had fulfilled a hundred and eleven years. Never did a tooth in his mouth hurt him, nor was his eyesight rendered less sharp, nor his body bent, nor his strength impaired; but he worked at his trade of a carpenter to the very last day of his life; and that was the six-and-twentieth of the month Abib.

30. And we apostles, when we heard these things from our Savior, rose up joyfully, and prostrated ourselves in honor of Him, and said: O our Savior, show us Thy grace. Now indeed we have heard the word of life: nevertheless we wonder, O our Savior, at the fate of Enoch and Elias, inasmuch as they had not to undergo death. For truly they dwell in the habitation of the righteous even to the present day, nor have their bodies seen corruption. Yet that old man Joseph the carpenter was, nevertheless, Thy father after the flesh. And Thou hast ordered us to go

into all the world and preach the holy Gospel; and Thou hast said: Relate to them the death of my father Joseph, and celebrate to him with annual solemnity a festival and sacred day. And whosoever shall take anything away from this narrative, or add anything to it, commits sin. We wonder especially that Joseph, even from that day on which Thou wast born in Bethlehem, called Thee his son after the flesh. Wherefore, then, didst Thou not make him immortal as well as them, and Thou sayest that he was righteous and chosen?

31. And our Saviour answered and said: Indeed, the prophecy of my Father upon Adam, for his disobedience, has now been fulfilled. And all things are arranged according to the will and pleasure of my Father. For if a man rejects the commandment of God, and follows the works of the devil by committing sin, his life is prolonged; for be is preserved in order that he may perhaps repent, and reflect that he must be delivered into the hands of death. But if any one has been zealous of good works, his life also is prolonged, that, as the fame of his old age increases, and upright men may imitate him. But when you see a man whose mind is prone to anger, assuredly his days are shortened; for it is these that are taken away in the flower of

their age. Every prophecy, therefore, which my Father has pronounced concerning the sons of men, must be fulfilled in every particular. But with reference to Enoch and Elias, and how they remain alive to this day, keeping the same bodies with which they were born; and as to what concerns my father Joseph, who has not been allowed as well as they to remain in the body: indeed, though a man live in the world many myriads of years, nevertheless at some time or other he is compelled to exchange life for death.

And I say to you, O my brethren, that they also, Enoch and Elias, must towards the end of time return into the world and die--in the day, namely, of commotion, of terror, of perplexity, and affliction. For Antichrist will slay four bodies, and will pour out their blood like water, because of the reproach to which they shall expose him, and the ignominy with which they, in their lifetime, shall brand him when they reveal his impiety.

32. And we said: O our Lord, our God and Savior, who are those four whom Thou hast said Antichrist will cut off from the reproach they bring upon him? The Lord answered: They are Enoch, Elias, Schila, and Tabitha. When we heard this from our Savior, we rejoiced and exulted; and we offered all

glory and thanksgiving to the Lord God, and our Savior Jesus Christ. He it is to whom is due glory, honor, dignity, dominion, power, and praise, as well as to the good Father with Him, and to the Holy Spirit that giveth life, henceforth and in all time for evermore. Amen.

The month Abib, is find in the Old Testament books of the Bible. Abib also known as the month of AV in the Jewish and is the seventh month of the modern Jewish civil year. Abib is August in our modern calendar.

Exodus 13:4

1.   And the LORD spake unto Moses, saying,
2.   Sanctify unto me all the firstborn, whatsoever openeth the womb among the children of Israel, *both* of man and of beast: it *is* mine.
3.   And Moses said unto the people, Remember this day, in which ye came out from Egypt, out of the house of bondage; for by strength of hand the LORD brought you out from this *place*: there shall no leavened bread be eaten.
4.   This day came ye out in the month Abib.

Exodus23:15

15   Thou shalt keep the feast of
unleavened bread: (thou shalt eat
unleavened bread seven days, as I
commanded thee, in the time appointed
of the month Abib; for in it thou camest
out from Egypt: and none shall appear
before me empty:)

Deuteronomy 16:1

1. Observe the month of Abib, and keep the
passover unto the LORD thy God: for in the
month of Abib the LORD thy God brought
thee forth out of Egypt by night.

Writes notes:

A. How old was Mary when Jesus was conceived?
Mary would have been around 14 years old when she conceived Jesus.

B. How old was Jesus when Joseph Died?
According to this and other records Jesus would have been around 18 years of age when Joseph the carpenter died

C. Did Jesus have any brother and sisters?
Jesus had fore half bothers, Named Judas, Justus, James the less and Simon
Jesus had two half sisters, Named Assia and Lydia

D. How old was Joseph when Jesus was born?
This book and other research all indicate Joseph was 93 years old.

E. How did Mary and Joseph meet?
The priests gave Mary to Joseph for him to take care of her.

Mary Conceives Jesus

Luke 1 :26-35

26   And in the sixth month the angel Gabriel was sent from God unto a city of Galilee, named Nazareth,

27   To a virgin espoused to a man whose name was Joseph, of the house of David; and the virgin's name *was* Mary.

28   And the angel came in unto her, and said, Hail, *thou that art* highly favored, the Lord *is* with thee: blessed *art* thou among women.

29   And when she saw *him,* she was troubled at his saying, and cast in her mind what manner of salutation this should be.

30   And the angel said unto her, Fear not, Mary: for thou hast found favour with God.

31   And, behold, thou shalt conceive in thy womb, and bring forth a son, and shalt call his name JESUS.

32   He shall be great, and shall be called the Son of the Highest: and the Lord God shall give unto him the throne of his father David:

33   And he shall reign over the house of Jacob for ever; and of his kingdom there shall be no end.

34   Then said Mary unto the angel, How shall this be, seeing I know not a man?

35   And the angel answered and said unto her, The Holy Ghost shall come upon thee, and the power of the Highest shall overshadow thee: therefore also that holy thing which shall be born of thee shall be called the Son of God.

Matthew 1:18-

18   Now the birth of Jesus Christ was on this wise: When as his mother Mary was espoused to Joseph, before they came together, she was found with child of the Holy Ghost.
19   Then Joseph her husband, being a just *man*, and not willing to make her a public example, was minded to put her away privily.
20   But while he thought on these things, behold, the angel of the Lord appeared unto him in a dream, saying, Joseph, thou son of David, fear not to take unto thee Mary thy wife: for that which is conceived in her is of the Holy Ghost.
21   And she shall bring forth a son, and thou shalt call his name JESUS: for he shall save his people from their sins.
22   Now all this was done, that it might be fulfilled which was spoken of the Lord by the prophet, saying,
23   Behold, a virgin shall be with child,

and shall bring forth a son, and they shall call his name Emmanuel, which being interpreted is, God with us.

24 Then Joseph being raised from sleep did as the angel of the Lord had bidden him, and took unto him his wife:

25 And knew her not till she had brought forth her firstborn son: and he called his name JESUS.

History of Josephs verse 6

6. But at mid-day there appeared to him in a dream the prince of the angels, the holy Gabriel, furnished with a command from my Father; and he said to him: Joseph, son of David, fear not to take Mary as your wife: for she has conceived of the Holy Spirit; and she will bring forth a son, whose name shall be called Jesus. He it is who shall rule all nations with a rod of iron. Having thus spoken, the angel departed from him. And Joseph rose from his sleep, and did as the angel of the Lord had said to him; and Mary abode with him.

Salome

Salome is found in **mark 15:40** at the crucifixion of Jesus.

40 There were also women looking on afar off: among whom was Mary Magdalene, and Mary the mother of

James the less and of Joses, and Salome;

Also in mark 16:1 Jesus is Risen.

1   And when the sabbath was past, Mary Magdalene, and Mary the *mother* of James, and Salome, had bought sweet spices, that they might come and anoint him.

The Death of Herod

No one knows for sure what killed Herod a great. However, from many descriptions in history of Herod's death, medical experts believe that hair and had kidney disease that was been complicated by a gangrene and record that the visible worms and putrefaction described in his final days are likely to have been scabies. Herod also suffered from depression and paranoia. Josephus said that herod was so concerned that no one would mourn his death that he gave orders to have distinguish men killed at the same time of his death so that the display of grief that he craved would take place.

Introduction:

We found in verse six of the history of Joseph and the carpenter, that Mary found James the less in his father's house broken-hearted and sad on account of the loss of his mother and Mary brought him up and is why Mary was called the mother James the less, James is the writer of this book the history of Mary the mother of Jesus. James the less is also the author of The book of James in the Bible

History of Mary the mother of Jesus

In the histories of the twelve tribes of Israel it is written that there was one Ioacim, exceeding rich: and he offered his gifts twofold, saying: That which is of my superfluity shall be for the whole people, and that which is for my forgiveness shall be for tile Lord, for a propitiation unto me.
 Now the great day of the Lord drew nigh and the children of Israel offered their gifts. And Reuben stood over against him saying: It is not lawful for thee to offer thy gifts first,-forasmuch as thou hast gotten no seed in Israel. And Ioacim was sore grieved, and went unto the record of the twelve tribes of the people, saying: I will look upon the record of the twelve tribes of Israel, whether I only have not gotten seed in Israel. And he searched, and found concerning all the righteous that they had raised up seed in Israel. And he remembered the

patriarch Abraham, how in the last days God gave him a son, even Isaac. And Ioacim was sore grieved, and showed not himself to his wife, but betook himself into the wilderness, and pitched his tent there, and fasted forty days and forty nights, saying within himself: I will not go down either for meat or for drink until the Lord my God visit me, and my prayer shall be unto me meat and drink.

Now his wife Anna lamented with two lamentations, and bewailed herself with two bewailing, saying: I will bewail my widowhood, and I will bewail my childlessness.

And the great day of the Lord drew nigh, and Judith her handmaid said unto her: How long humblest thou thy soul? The great day of the Lord hath come, and it is not lawful for thee to mourn: but take this headband, which the mistress of my work gave me, and it is not lawful for me to put it on, forasmuch as I am an handmaid, and it hath a mark of royalty. And Anna said: Get thee from me. Lo! I have done nothing (or I will not do so) and the Lord hath greatly humbled me: peradventure one gave it to thee in subtilty, and thou art come to make me partaker in thy sin. And Judith said: How shall I curse thee, seeing the Lord hath shut up thy womb, to give thee no fruit in Israel?

And Anna was sore grieved [and mourned with a great mourning because she was reproached by all the tribes of Israel. And coming to herself she said: What shall I do? I will pray with weeping unto the Lord my God that he visits me]. And she put off her mourning garments and cleansed (or adorned) her head and put on her bridal garments: and about the ninth hour she went down into the garden to walk there. And she saw a laurel-tree and sat down underneath it and besought the Lord saying: O God of our fathers, bless me, and hearken unto my prayer, as thou didst bless the womb of Sarah, and gavest her a son, even Isaac.

And looking up to the heaven she espied a nest of sparrows in the laurel-tree, and made a lamentation within herself, saying: Woe unto me, who begat me ? And what womb brought me forth for I am become a curse before the children of Israel, and I am reproached, and they have mocked me forth out of the temple of the Lord? Woe unto me, unto what am I likened ? I am not likened unto the fowls of the heaven, for even the fowls of the heaven are fruitful before thee, O Lord. Woe unto me, unto what am I likened? I am not likened unto the beasts of the earth, for even the beasts of the earth are fruitful before thee, O Lord. Woe unto me, unto what am I likened? I am not likened unto these waters, for even these waters are fruitful before thee, O Lord. Woe unto me, unto what am I likened? I am not likened unto this earth, for even this earth bringeth forth her fruits in due season and blesseth thee, O Lord.

And behold an angel of the Lord appeared, saying unto her: Anna, Anna, the Lord hath hearkened unto thy prayer, and thou shalt conceive and bear, and thy seed shall be spoken of in the whole world. And Anna said: As the Lord my God liveth, if I bring forth either male or female, I will bring it for a gift unto the Lord my God, and it shall be ministering unto him all the days of its life.

And behold there came two messengers saying unto her: Behold Ioacim thy husband cometh with his flocks: for an angel of the Lord came down unto him saying: Ioacim, Ioacim, the Lord God hath hearkened unto thy prayer. Get thee down hence, for behold thy wife Anna hath conceived. And

Ioacim sat him down and called his herdsmen saying: Bring me hither ten lambs without blemish and without spot, and they shall be for the Lord my God; and bring me twelve tender calves, and they shall be for the priests and for the assembly of the elders; and an hundred kids for the whole people.

And behold Ioacim came with his flocks, and Anna stood at the gate and saw Ioacim coming, and ran and hung upon his neck, saying: Now know I that the Lord God hath greatly blessed me: for behold the widow is no more a widow, and she that was childless shall conceive. And Ioacim rested the first day in his house.

And on the morrow he offered his gifts, saying in himself: If the Lord God be reconciled unto me, the plate that is upon the forehead of the priest will make it manifest unto me. And Ioacim offered his gifts and looked earnestly upon the plate of the priest when he went up unto the altar of tile Lord, and he saw no sin in himself. And Ioacim said: Now know I that the Lord is become propitious unto me and hath forgiven all my sins. And he went down from the temple of the Lord justified, and went unto his house.

And her months were fulfilled, and in the ninth month Anna brought forth. And she said unto the midwife: what have I brought forth ? And she said: A female. And Anna said: My soul is magnified this day, and she laid herself down. And when the days were fulfilled, Anna purified herself and gave suck to the child and called her name Mary.

And day by day the child waxed strong, and when she was six months old her mother stood her upon the ground to try if she would stand; and she walked seven steps and returned unto her bosom. And she caught her up, saying: As the Lord my God liveth, thou shalt walk no more upon this ground, until I bring thee into the temple of the Lord. And she made a sanctuary in her bed chamber and suffered nothing common or unclean to pass through it. And she called for the daughters of the Hebrews that were undefiled, and they carried her hither and thither.

And the first year of the child was fulfilled, and Ioacim made a great feast and bade the priests and the scribes and the assembly of the elders and the whole people of Israel. And Ioacim brought the child to the priests, and they blessed her, saying: 0 God of our fathers, bless this child and give her a name renowned for ever among all generations. And all the people said: So be it, so be it. Amen. And he brought her to the high priests, and they blessed her, saying: 0 God of the high places, look upon this child, and bless her with the last blessing which hath no successor.

And her mother caught her up into the sanctuary of her bed chamber and gave her suck.

And Anna made a song unto the Lord God, saying: I will sing an hymn unto the Lord my God, because he hath visited me and taken away from me the reproach of mine enemies, and the Lord hath given me a fruit of his righteousness, single and manifold before him. Who shall declare unto the sons of Reuben that Anna giveth suck? Hearken, hearken, ye twelve tribes of Israel, that Anna giveth suck. And she laid the child to rest in the bed chamber of her sanctuary, and went forth and ministered unto them. And when the feast was ended, they gat them down rejoicing, and glorifying the God of Israel.

And unto the child her months were added: and the child became two years old. And Ioacim said: Let us bring her up to the temple of the Lord that we

may pay the promise which we promised; lest the
Lord require it of us (lit. send unto us), and our gift
become unacceptable. And Anna said: Let us wait
until the third year, that the child may not long after
her father or mother. And Ioacim said: Let us wait.

And the child became three years old, and Ioacim
said: Call for the daughters of the Hebrews that are
undefiled and let them take every one a lamp, and
let them be burning, that the child turn not
backward and her heart be taken captive away from
the temple of the Lord. And they did so until they
were gone up into the temple of the Lord.
And the priest received her and kissed her and
blessed her and said: The Lord hath magnified thy
name among all generations: in thee in the latter
days shall the Lord make manifest his redemption
unto the children of Israel. And he made her to sit
upon the third step of the altar. And the Lord put
grace upon her and she danced with her feet and all
tile house of Israel loved her.

And her parents gat them down marveling, and
praising the Lord God because tile child was not
turned away backward.
And Mary was in the temple of the Lord as a dove
that is nurtured: and she received food from the
hand of an angel.

And when she was twelve years old, there was a
council of the priests, saying: Behold Mary is
become twelve years old in the temple of the Lord.
What then shall we do with her ? lest she pollute the
sanctuary of the Lord. And they said unto the high
priest: Thou standest over the altar of the Lord.
Enter in and pray concerning her: And whatsoever
the Lord shall reveal to thee, that let us do.

And the high priest took the vestment with the
twelve bells and went in unto the Holy of Holies

and prayed concerning her. And lo, an angel of tile Lord appeared saying unto him: Zacharias, Zacharias go forth and assemble them that are widowers of the people, and let them bring every man a rod, and to whomsoever the Lord shall show a sign, his wife shall she be. And the heralds went forth over all the country round about Judaea, and the trumpet of the Lord sounded, and all men ran thereto.

And Joseph cast down his adze and ran to meet them, and when they were gathered together they went to the high priest and took their rods with them. And he took the rods of them all and went into the temple and prayed. And when he had finished the prayer he took the rods and went forth and gave them back to them: and there was no sign upon them. But Joseph received the last rod: and lo, a dove came forth of the rod and flew upon the bead of Joseph. And the priest said unto Joseph: Unto thee hath it fallen to take the virgin of the Lord and keep her for thyself.   And Joseph refused, saying: I have sons, and I am an old man, but she is a girl: lest I became a laughing-stock to the children of Israel. And the priest said unto Joseph: Year the Lord thy God, and remember what things God did unto Dathan and Abiram and Korah, how the earth clave and they were swallowed up because of their gainsaying. And now fear thou, Joseph, lest it be so in thine house. And Joseph was afraid, and took her to keep her for himself. And Joseph said unto Mary: Lo, I have received thee out of the temple of the Lord: and now do I leave thee in my house, and I go away to build my buildings and I will come again unto thee. The Lord shall watch over thee.

Now there was a council of the priests, and they said: Let us make a veil for the temple of the Lord.

And the priest said: Call unto me pure virgins of the tribe of David. And the officers departed and sought and found seven virgins. And the
priests called to mind the child Mary, that she was of the tribe of avid and was undefiled before God: and the officers went and fetched her. And they brought them into the temple of the Lord, and the priest said: Cast me lots, which of you shah weave the gold and the undefiled (the white) and tile fine linen and the silk and the hyacinthine, and the scarlet and the true purple. And the lot of the true purple and the scarlet fell unto Mary, and she took them and went unto her house.
[And at that season Zacharias became dumb, and Samuel was
in his stead until the time when Zacharias spake again.]But Mary took the scarlet and began to spin it.

And she took the pitcher and went forth to fill it with water: and lo a voice saying: Hail, thou that art highly favored; the Lord is with thee: blessed art thou among women.
And she looked about her upon the right hand and upon the left, to see whence this voice should be: and being filled with trembling she~ went to her house and set down the pitcher, and took the purple and sat down upon her seat and drew out the thread.

And behold an angel of the Lord stood before her saying: Fear not, Mary, for thou hast found grace before the Lord of all things, and thou shalt conceive of his word. And she, when she heard it, questioned in herself, saying: Shall I verily conceive of the living God, and bring forth after the manner of all women? And the angel of the Lord said: Not so, Mary, for a power of the Lord shall overshadow thee: wherefore also that holy thing which shall be

born of thee shall be called the Son of the Highest.
And thou shalt call his name Jesus: for he shall save
his people from their sins. And Mary said: Behold
the handmaid of the Lord is before him: be it unto
me according to thy word.

And she made the purple and the scarlet and
brought them unto the priest. And the priest blessed
her and said: Mary, the Lord God hath magnified
thy name, and thou shalt be blessed among all
generations of the earth. And Mary rejoiced and
went away unto Elizabeth her kinswoman: and she
knocked at the door. And Elizabeth when she heard
it cast down the scarlet (al. the wool) and ran to the
door and opened it, and when she saw Mary she
blessed her and said: Whence is this to me that the
mother of my Lord should come unto me? For
behold that which is in me leaped and blessed thee.
And Mary forgot the mysteries which Gabriel the
archangel had told her, and she looked up unto the
heaven and said: Who am I, Lord, that all the
generations of the earth do bless me? And she
abode three months with Elizabeth, and day by day
her womb grew: and Mary was afraid and departed
unto her house and hid herself from the children of
Israel. Now she was sixteen years old when these
mysteries came to pass.

Now it was the sixth month with her, and behold
Joseph came from his building, and he entered into
his house and found her great with child. And he
smote his face, and cast himself down upon the
ground on sackcloth and wept bitterly, saying: With
what countenance shall I look unto the Lord my
God ? and what prayer shall I make concerning this
maiden? for I received her out of the temple of the
Lord my God a virgin, and have not kept her safe.
Who is he that hath ensnared me ? Who hath done

this evil in mine house and hath defiled the virgin ?
Is not the story of Adam repeated in me ? for as at
the hour of his giving thanks the serpent came and
found Eve alone and deceived her, so hath it
befallen me also. And Joseph arose from off the
sackcloth and called Mary and said unto her O thou
that wast cared for by God, why hast thou done this
? thou hast forgotten the Lord thy God. Why hast
thou humbled thy soul, thou that wast nourished up
in the Holy of Holies and didst receive food at the
hand of an angel? But she wept bitterly, saying: I
am pure and I know not a man. And Joseph said
unto her: Whence then is that which is in thy womb
? and she said: As the Lord my God liveth, I know
not whence it is come unto me.

And Joseph was sore afraid and ceased from
speaking unto her (or left her alone), and pondered
what he should do with her. And Joseph said: If I
hide her sin, I shall be found fighting against the
law of the Lord: and if I manifest her unto the
children of Israel, I fear lest that which is in her be
the seed of an angel, and I shall be found delivering
up innocent blood to the judgment of death. What
then shall I do? I will let her go from me privily.
And the night came upon him. And behold an angel
of the Lord appeared unto him in a dream, saying:
Fear not this child, for that which is in her is of the
Holy Ghost, and she shall bear a son and thou shalt
call his name Jesus, for he shall save his people
from their sins. And Joseph arose from sleep and
glorified the God of Israel which had shown this
favor unto her: and he watched over her.

Now Annas the scribe came unto him and said to
him: Wherefore didst thou not appear in our
assembly ? and Joseph said unto him: I was weary
with the journey, and I rested the first day. And

Annas turned him about and saw Mary great with
child. And he went hastily to the priest and said
unto him: Joseph, to whom thou bearest witness
[that he is righteous] hath sinned grievously. And
the priest said: Wherein? And he said: The virgin
whom he received out of the temple of the Lord, he
hath defiled her, and married her by stealth (lit.
stolen her marriage), and hath not declared it to the
children of Israel. And the priest answered and said:
Hath Joseph done this? And Annas the scribe said:
Send officers and thou shalt find the virgin great
with child. And the officers went and found as he
had said, and they brought her together with Joseph
unto the place of judgment. And the priest said:
Mary, wherefore hast thou done this, and wherefore
hast thou humbled thy soul and forgotten the Lord
thy God, thou that wast nurtured in the Holy of
Holies and didst receive food at the hand of an
angel and didst hear the hymns and didst dance
before the Lord, wherefore hast thou done this?
But she wept bitterly, saying: As the Lord my God
liveth I am pure before him and I know not a man. 4
And the priest said unto Joseph: Wherefore hast
thou done this? And Joseph said: As the Lord my
God liveth I am pure as concerning her. And the
priest said: Bear no false witness but speak the
truth: thou hast married her by stealth and hast not
declared it unto the children of Israel, and hast not
bowed thine head under the mighty hand that thy
seed should be blessed. And Joseph held his peace.
 and the priest said: Restore the virgin whom thou
didst receive out of the temple of the Lord. And
Joseph was full of weeping. And the priest said: I
will give you to drink of the water of the conviction
of the Lord, and it will make manifest your sins
before your eyes. And the priest took thereof and

made Joseph drink and sent him into the hill-country. And he returned whole. He made Mary also drink and sent her into the hill-country. And she returned whole. And all the people marvelled, because sin appeared not in them. And the priest said: If the Lord God hath not made your sin manifest, neither do I condemn you. And he let them go. And Joseph took Mary and departed unto his house rejoicing, and glorifying the God of Israel.

Now there went out a decree from Augustus the king that all that were in Bethlehem of Judaea should be recorded. And Joseph said: I will record my sons: but this child, what shall I do with her ? how shall I record her ? as my wife ? nay, I am ashamed. Or as my daughter? but all the children of Israel know that she is not my daughter. This day of the Lord shall do as the Lord willeth. And he saddled the she-ass, and set her upon it, and his son led it and Joseph followed after. And they drew near (unto Bethlehem) within three miles: and Joseph turned himself about and saw her of a sad countenance and said within himself: Peradventure that which is within her paineth her. And again Joseph turned himself about and saw her laughing, and said unto her: Mary, what aileth thee that I see thy face at one time laughing and at another time sad ? And Mary said unto Joseph: It is because I behold two peoples with mine eyes, the one weeping and lamenting and the other rejoicing and exulting.

And they came to the midst of the way, and Mary said unto him: Take me down from the ass, for that which is within me presseth me, to come forth. And he took her down from the ass and said unto her: Whither shall I take thee to hide thy shame? For the place is desert.

And he found a cave there and brought her into it, and set his sons by her: and he went forth and sought for a midwife of the Hebrews in the country of Bethlehem.

Now I Joseph was walking, and I walked not. And I looked up to the air and saw the air in amazement. And I looked up unto the pole of the heaven and saw it standing still, and the fowls of the heaven without motion. And I looked upon the earth and saw a dish set, and workmen lying by it, and their hands were in the dish: and they that were chewing chewed not, and they that were lifting the food lifted it not, and they that put it to their mouth put it not thereto, but the faces of all of them were looking upward. And behold there were sheep being driven, and they went not forward but stood still; and the shepherd lifted his hand to smite them with his staff, and his hand remained up. And I looked upon the stream of the river and saw the mouths of the kids upon the water and they drank not. And of a sudden all things moved onward in their course.

And behold a woman coming down from the hillcountry, and she said to me: Man, whither goest thou ? And I said: I seek a midwife of the Hebrews. And she answered and said unto me: Art thou of Israel ? And I said unto her: Yea. And she said: And who is she that bringeth forth in the cave ? And I said: She that is betrothed unto me. And she said to me: Is she not thy wife? And I said to her: It is Mary that was nurtured up in the temple of the Lord: and I received her to wife by lot: and she is not my wife, but she hath conception by the Holy Ghost.

And the midwife said unto him: Is this the truth? And Joseph said unto her: Come hither and see. And the midwife went with him.

And they stood in the place of the cave: and behold a bright cloud overshadowing the cave. And the midwife said: My soul is magnified this day, because mine eyes have seen marvellous things: for salvation is born unto Israel. And immediately the cloud withdrew itself out of the cave, and a great light appeared in the cave so that our eyes could not endure it. And by little and little that light withdrew itself until the young child appeared: and it went and took the breast of its mother Mary.
And the midwife cried aloud and said: Great unto me to-day is this day, in that ! have seen this new sight.   And the midwife went forth of the cave and Salome met her. And she said to her: Salome, Salome, a new sight have I to tell thee. A virgin hath brought forth, which her nature alloweth not. And Salome said: As the Lord my God liveth, if I make not trial and prove her nature I will not believe that a virgin hath brought forth.

And the midwife went in and said unto Mary: Order thyself, for there is no small contention arisen concerning thee. Arid Salome made trial and cried out and said: Woe unto mine iniquity and mine unbelief, because I have tempted the living God, and lo, my hand falleth away from me in fire. And she bowed her knees unto the Lord, saying: O God of my fathers, remember that I am the seed of Abraham and Isaac and Jacob: make me not a public example unto the children of Israel, but restore me unto the poor, for thou knowest, Lord, that in thy name did I perform my cures, and did receive my hire of thee.   And lo, an angel of the Lord appeared, saying unto her: Salome, Salome, the Lord hath hearkened to thee: bring thine hand near unto the young child and take him up, and there shall be unto thee salvation and joy.   And

Salome came near and took him up, saying: I will
do him worship, for a great king is born unto Israel.
And behold immediately Salome was healed: and
she went forth of the cave justified. And Io, a voice
saying: Salome, Salome, tell none of the marvels
which thou hast seen, until the child enter into
Jerusalem.

And behold, Joseph made him ready to go forth
into Judaea. And there came a great tumult in
Bethlehem of Judaea; for there came wise men,
saying: Where is he that is born king of the Jews?
for we have seen his star in the east and arc come to
worship him. And when Herod heard it he was
troubled and sent officers unto the wise men. And
he sent for the high priests and examined them,
saying: How is it written concerning the Christ,
where he is born? They say unto him: In Bethlehem
of Judaea: for so it is written. And he let them go.
And he examined the wise men, saying unto them:
What sign saw ye concerning the king that is born?
And the wise men said: We saw a very great star
shining among those stars and dimming them so
that the stars appeared not: and thereby knew we
that a king was born unto Israel, and we came to
worship him. And Herod said: Go and seek for him,
and if ye find him, tell me, that I also may come and
worship him. And the wise men went forth. And lo,
the star which they saw in the east went before them
until they entered into the cave: and it stood over
the head of the cave. And the wise men saw the
young child with Mary, his mother: and they
brought out of their scrip gifts, gold-and
frankincense and myrrh. And being warned by the
angel that they should not enter into Judaea, they
went into their own country by another way.

But when Herod perceived that he was mocked by the wise men, he was wroth, and sent murderers, saying unto them: Slay the children from two years old and under. And when Mary heard that the children were being slain, she was afraid, and took the young child and wrapped in swaddling clothes and laid him in an ox-manger.

But Elizabeth when she heard that they sought for John took him and went up into the hill-country and looked about her where she should hide him: and there was no hiding-place. And Elizabeth groaned and said with a loud voice: 0 mountain of God, receive thou a mother with a child. For Elizabeth was not able to go up. And immediately the mountain clave asunder and took her in. And there was a light shining alway for them: for an angel of the Lord was with them, keeping watch over them.

Now Herod sought for John, and sent officers to Zacharias, saying: Where hast thou hidden thy son? And he answered and said unto them: I am a minister of God and attend continually upon the temple of the Lord: I know not where my son is. And the officers departed and told Herod all these things. And Herod was wroth and said: His son is to be king over Israel. And he sent unto him again, saying: Say the truth: where is thy son? for thou knowest that thy blood is under my hand. And the officers departed and told him all these things. And Zacharias said: I am a martyr of God if thou sheddest my blood: for my spirit the Lord shah receive, because thou sheddest innocent blood in the fore-court of the temple of the Lord.

And about the dawning of the day Zacharias was slain. And the children of Israel knew not that he was slain.

But the priests entered in at the hour of the salutation, and the blessing of Zacharias met them not according to the manner. And the priests stood waiting for Zacharias, to salute him with the prayer, and to glorify the Most High. But as he delayed to come, they were all afraid: and one of them took courage and entered in: and he saw beside the altar congealed blood: and a voice saying: Zacharias hath been slain, and his blood shall not be wiped out until his avenger come. And when he heard that word he was afraid, and went forth and told the priests. And they took courage and went in and saw that which was done: and the panels of the temple did wail: and they rent their clothes from the top to the bottom. And his body they found not, but his blood they found turned into stone. And they feared, and went forth and told all the people that Zacharias was slain. And all tile tribes of the people heard it, and they mourned for him and lamented him three days and three nights. And after the three days the priests took counsel whom they should set in his stead: and the lot came up upon Symeon. Now he it was which was warned by the Holy Ghost that he should not see death until he should see the Christ in the flesh.

Now I, James, which wrote this history in Jerusalem, when there arose a tumult when Herod died, withdrew myself into the wilderness until the tumult ceased in Jerusalem.
Glorifying the Lord God which gave me the gift, and the wisdom to write this history.

And grace shall be with those that fear our Lord Jesus Christ: to whom be glory for ever and ever. Amen.

Jesus birth foretold

The book of Luke chapter 1: 26-38

26   And in the sixth month the angel Gabriel was sent from God unto a city of Galilee, named Nazareth,

27   To a virgin espoused to a man whose name was Joseph, of the house of David; and the virgin's name *was* Mary.

28   And the angel came in unto her, and said, Hail, *thou that art* highly favoured, the Lord *is* with thee: blessed *art* thou among women.

29   And when she saw *him*, she was troubled at his saying, and cast in her mind what manner of salutation this should be.

30   And the angel said unto her, Fear not, Mary: for thou hast found favour with God.

31   And, behold, thou shalt conceive in thy womb, and bring forth a son, and shalt call his name JESUS.

32   He shall be great, and shall be called the Son of the Highest: and the Lord God shall give unto him the throne of his father David:

33   And he shall reign over the house of Jacob for ever; and of his kingdom there shall be no end.

34   Then said Mary unto the angel, How shall this be, seeing I know not a man?

35　And the angel answered and said unto her, The Holy Ghost shall come upon thee, and the power of the Highest shall overshadow thee: therefore also that holy thing which shall be born of thee shall be called the Son of God.

36　And, behold, thy cousin Elisabeth, she hath also conceived a son in her old age: and this is the sixth month with her, who was called barren.

37　For with God nothing shall be impossible.

38　And Mary said, Behold the handmaid of the Lord; be it unto me according to thy word. And the angel departed from her.

Mary Visits Elizabeth

39　¶ And Mary arose in those days, and went into the hill country with haste, into a city of Juda;

40　And entered into the house of Zacharias, and saluted Elisabeth.

41　And it came to pass, that, when Elisabeth heard the salutation of Mary, the babe leaped in her womb; and Elisabeth was filled with the Holy Ghost:

42　And she spake out with a loud voice, and said, Blessed *art* thou among women, and blessed *is* the fruit of thy womb.

43 And whence *is* this to me, that the mother of my Lord should come to me?

44 For, lo, as soon as the voice of thy salutation sounded in mine ears, the babe leaped in my womb for joy.

45 And blessed *is* she that believed: for there shall be a performance of those things which were told her from the Lord.

46 And Mary said, My soul doth magnify the Lord,

47 And my spirit hath rejoiced in God my Saviour.

48 For he hath regarded the low estate of his handmaiden: for, behold, from henceforth all generations shall call me blessed.

49 For he that is mighty hath done to me great things; and holy *is* his name.

50 And his mercy *is* on them that fear him from generation to generation.

51 He hath shewed strength with his arm; he hath scattered the proud in the imagination of their hearts.

52 He hath put down the mighty from *their* seats, and exalted them of low degree.

53 He hath filled the hungry with good things; and the rich he hath sent empty away.

54 He hath holpen his servant Israel, in remembrance of *his* mercy;

55   As he spake to our fathers, to Abraham, and to his seed for ever.

Let us take note of verse 56

56   And Mary abode with her about three months, and returned to her own house.

We see here in the book of Luke that Mary stayed with Elizabeth for about three months, and then returned home. So we find in verse 5 of the history of Joseph the carpenter. (Three months after Mary's conception the righteous man Joseph returned from the place where he worked at his trade. And when he found Mary a virgin pregnant) Mary stayed with Elizabeth until it was time for Joseph to return home.

Writes notes:

6. Who was Mary's Parents?
> Loacim and Anna

7. Why was John the Baptist, not killed by Herod the Great?
> Elizabeth when she heard that they sought for her child john she took him, Went up into the hill country. And looked about her where she

should hide him, and there was no hiding places and Elizabeth groaned and said with a loud voice: O mountain of God, receive thou a mother with a child. For Elizabeth was not able to go up. And immediately the mountain clave asunder and took her in. and there was a light shining always for them. For an angel of the lord was with them, keeping watch over them.

Introduction

The following Book is also one of the ancient writings find in the Archives, the book was written by the apostle John about Mary The mother of Jesus death. So I felt it was important to include this writing in the book.

Departure of Mary the mother of Jesus to Heaven

Holy glorious Mother of God and ever-virgin Mary, as was her wont, was going to the holy tomb of our Lord to burn incense, and bending her holy knees, she was importunate that Christ our God who had

been born of her should return to her. And
the Jews, seeing her lingering by the divine
sepulchre, came to the chief priests, saying:
Mary goes every day to the tomb. And the
chief priests, having summoned the guards
set by them not to allow any one to pray at
the holy sepulchre, inquired about her,
whether in truth it were so. And the guards
answered and said that they had seen no
such thing, God having not allowed them to
see her when there. And on one of the days,
it being the preparation, the holy Mary, as
was her wont, came to the sepulchre; and
while she was praying, it came to pass that
the heavens were opened, and the archangel
Gabriel came down to her and said: *Hail,
thou that didst bring forth Christ our God!
Thy prayer having come through to the
heavens to Him who was born of thee, has
been accepted; and from this time,
according to thy request, thou having left the
world, shall go to the heavenly places to thy
Son, into the true and everlasting life.*
And having heard this from the holy
archangel, she returned to holy Bethlehem,
having along with her three virgins who
ministered unto her. And after having rested
a short time, she sat up and said to the
virgins: Bring me a censer, that I may pray.
And they brought it, as they had been
commanded. And she prayed, saying: My

Lord Jesus Christ, who didst deign through Thy supreme goodness to be born of me, hear my voice, and send me Thy apostle John, in order that, seeing him, I may partake of joy; and send me also the rest of Thy apostles, both those who have already gone to Thee, and those in the world that now is, in whatever country they may be, through Thy holy commandment, in order that, having beheld them, I may bless Thy name much to be praised; for I am confident that Thou hearest Thy servant in everything. And while she was praying, I John came, the Holy Spirit having snatched me up by a cloud from Ephesus, and set me in the place where the mother of my Lord was lying. And having gone in beside her, and glorified Him who had been born of her, I said: Hail, mother of my Lord, who didst bring forth Christ our God, rejoice that in great glory thou art going out of this life. And the holy mother of God glorified God, because I John had come to her, remembering the voice of the Lord, saying: Behold thy mother, and, Behold thy son. And the three virgins came and worshipped. And the holy mother of God says to me: Pray, and cast incense. And I prayed thus: Lord Jesus Christ, who hast done wonderful things, now also do wonderful things before her who brought Thee forth; and let Thy mother depart from this life; and let those who crucified Thee, and who have not believed in Thee, be confounded. And after I had ended the prayer, holy Mary said to me: Bring me the censer. And having cast incense, she said, Glory to Thee, my God and my Lord, because there has been fulfilled in me whatsoever Thou didst promise to me before thou didst ascend into the heavens, that when I should depart from this world Thou wouldst come to me, and the multitude of Thine angels, with glory. And I John say to her: Jesus Christ our Lord and our God is coming and thou seest Him, as He promised to thee. And the holy mother of God answered and said to me: The Jews have sworn that after I have died they will burn my body. And I answered and said to her: Thy holy and precious body will by no means see corruption. And she answered and said to me: Bring a censer, and cast incense, and pray. And there came a voice out of the heavens saying the Amen. And I John heard this voice; and the Holy Spirit said to me: John, hast thou heard this voice that spoke in the heaven after the prayer was ended? And I answered and said: Yes, I heard. And the Holy Spirit said to me: This voice which thou didst hear denotes that the appearance of thy brethren the apostles is at hand, and of the holy powers that they are coming hither to-day. And at this I John prayed.

And the Holy Spirit said to the apostles: Let all of you together, having come by the clouds from the ends of the world, be assembled to holy Bethlehem by a whirlwind, on account of the mother of our Lord Jesus Christ; Peter from Rome, Paul from Tiberia, Thomas from Hither India, James from Jerusalem. Andrew, Peter's brother, and Philip, Luke, and Simon the Cananaean, and Thaddaeus who had fallen asleep, were raised by the Holy Spirit out of their tombs; to whom the Holy Spirit said: Do not think that it is now the resurrection; but on this account you have risen out of your tombs, that you may go to give greeting to the honor and wonder-working of the mother of our Lord and Savior Jesus Christ, because the day of her departure is at hand, of her going up into the heavens. And Mark likewise coming round, was present from Alexandria; he also with the rest, as has been said before, from each country. And Peter being lifted up by a cloud, stood between heaven and earth, the Holy Spirit keeping him steady. And at the same time, the rest of the apostles also, having been snatched up in clouds, were found along with Peter. And thus by the Holy Spirit, as has been said, they all came together.

And having gone in beside the mother of our Lord and God, and having adored, we said: Fear not, nor grieve; God the Lord, who was born of thee, will take thee out of this world with glory. And rejoicing in God her Savior, she sat up in the bed, and says to the apostles: Now have I believed that our Master and God is coming from heaven, and I shall behold Him, and thus depart from this life, as I have seen that you have come. And I wish you to tell me how you knew that I was departing and came to me, and from what countries and through what distance you have come hither, that you have thus made haste to visit me. For neither has He who was born of me, our Lord Jesus Christ, the God of the universe, concealed it; for I am persuaded even now that He is the Son of the Most High.

And Peter answered and said to the apostles: Let us each, according to what the Holy Spirit announced and commanded us, give full information to the mother of our Lord. And I John answered and said: Just as I was going in to the holy altar in Ephesus to perform divine service, the Holy Spirit says to me, The time of the departure of the mother of thy Lord is at hand; go to Bethlehem to salute her. And a cloud of light snatched me up, and set me down in the door where thou art lying. Peter also answered: And I, living in Rome, about dawn heard a voice through the Holy Spirit saying to me, The mother of thy Lord is to depart, as the time is at hand; go to Bethlehem to salute her. And, behold, a cloud of light snatched me up; and I beheld also the other apostles coming to me on clouds, and a voice saying to me, Go all to Bethlehem. And Paul also answered and said: And I, living in a city at no great distance from Rome, called the country of Tiberia, heard the Holy Spirit saying to me, The mother of thy Lord, having left this world, is making her course to the celestial regions through her departure; but go thou also to Bethlehem to salute her. And, behold, a cloud of light having snatched me up, set me down in the same place as you. And Thomas also answered and said: And I, traversing the country of the Indians, when the preaching was prevailing by the grace of Christ, and the king's sister's son Labdanus by name, was about to be sealed by me in the palace, on a sudden the Holy Spirit says to me, Do thou also, Thomas, go to Bethlehem to salute the mother of thy Lord, because she is taking her departure to the heavens. And a cloud of light having snatched me up, set me down beside you. And Mark also answered and said: And when I was finishing the canon of the third day in the city of Alexandria, just as I was praying, the Holy Spirit snatched me up, and brought me to you. And James also answered and said: While I was in Jerusalem, the Holy Spirit commanded me, saying, Go to Bethlehem, because the mother of thy Lord is taking her departure. And, behold, a cloud of light having snatched me up, set me beside you. And Matthew also answered and said: I have glorified and do glorify God, because when I was in a boat and overtaken by a storm, the sea raging with its waves, on a sudden a cloud of light overshadowing the stormy billow, changed it to a calm, and having snatched me up, set me down beside you. And those who had come before likewise answered, and gave an account of how they had come. And Bartholomew said: I was in the Thebais proclaiming the word, and behold the Holy Spirit says to me, The mother of thy Lord is taking her departure; go, then, to salute her in Bethlehem. And, behold, a cloud of light having snatched me up, brought me to you.

The apostles said all these things to the holy mother of God, why they had come, and in what way; and she stretched her hands to heaven and prayed, saying: I adore, and praise, and glorify Thy much to he praised name, O Lord, because Thou hast looked upon the lowliness of Thine handmaiden, and because Thou that art mighty hast done great things for me; and, behold, all generations shall count me blessed. And after the prayer she said to the apostles: Cast incense, and pray. And when they had prayed, there was thunder from heaven, and there came a fearful voice, as if of chariots; and, behold, a multitude of a host of angels and powers, and a voice, as if of the Son of man, was heard, and the seraphim in a circle round the house where the holy, spotless mother of God and virgin was lying, so that all who were in Bethlehem beheld all the wonderful things, and came to Jerusalem and reported all the wonderful things that had come to pass. And it came to pass, when the voice was heard, that the sun and the moon suddenly appeared about the house; and an assembly of the first-born saints stood beside the house where the mother of the Lord was lying, for her honour and glory. And I beheld also that many signs came to pass, the blind seeing, the deaf hearing, the lame walking, lepers cleansed, and those possessed by unclean spirits cured; and every one who was under disease and sickness, touching the outside of the wall of the house where she was lying, cried out: Holy Mary, who didst bring forth Christ our God, have mercy upon us. And they were straightway cured. And great multitudes out of every country living in Jerusalem for the sake of prayer, having heard of the signs that had come to pass in Bethlehem through the mother of the Lord, came to the place seeking the cure of various diseases, which also they obtained. And there was joy unspeakable on that day among the multitude of those who had been cured, as well as of those who looked on, glorifying Christ our God and His mother. And all Jerusalem from Bethlehem kept festival with psalms and spiritual songs. And the priests of the Jews, along with their people, were astonished at the things which had come to pass; and being moved with the heaviest hatred, and again with frivolous reasoning, having made an assembly, they determine to send against the holy mother of God and the holy apostles who were there in Bethlehem. And accordingly the multitude of the Jews, having directed their course to Bethlehem, when at the distance of one mile it came to pass that they beheld a frightful vision, and their feet were held fast; and after this they returned to their fellow-countrymen, and reported all the frightful vision to the chief priests. And they, still more boiling with rage, go to the procurator, crying out and saying: The nation of the Jews has been ruined by this woman; chase her from Bethlehem and the province of Jerusalem. And the procurator, astonished at the wonderful things, said to them: I will chase her neither from Bethlehem nor from any other place. And the Jews continued crying out, and adjuring him by the health of Tiberius Caesar to bring the apostles out of Bethlehem. And if you do not do so, we shall report it to the Caesar. Accordingly, being compelled, he sends a tribune of the soldiers against the apostles to Bethlehem. And the Holy Spirit says to the apostles and the mother of the Lord: Behold, the procurator has sent a tribune against you, the Jews having made an uproar. Go forth therefore from Bethlehem, and fear not: for, behold, by a cloud I shall bring you to Jerusalem; for the power of the Father, and the Son, and the Holy Spirit is with you. The apostles therefore rose up immediately, and went forth from the house, carrying the bed of the Lady the mother of God, and directed their course to Jerusalem; and immediately, as the Holy Spirit had said, being lifted up by a cloud, they were found in Jerusalem in the house of the Lady. And they stood up, and for five days made an unceasing singing of praise. And when the tribune came to Bethlehem, and found there neither the mother of the Lord nor the apostles, he laid hold of the Bethlehemites, saying to them:

Did you not come telling the procurator and the priests all the signs and wonders that had come to pass, and how the apostles had come out of every country? Where are they, then? Come; go to the procurator at Jerusalem. For the tribune did not know of the departure of the apostles and the Lord's mother to Jerusalem. The tribune then, having taken the Bethlehemites, went in to the procurator, saying that he had found no one. And after five days it was known to the procurator, and the priests. and all the city, that the Lord's mother was in her own house in Jerusalem, along with the apostles, from the signs and wonders that came to pass there. And a multitude of men and women and virgins came together, and cried out: Holy virgin, that didst bring forth Christ our God, do not forget the generation of men. And when these things came to pass, the people of the Jews, with the priests also, being the more moved with hatred, took wood and fire, and came up, wishing to burn the house where the Lord's mother was living with the apostles. And the procurator stood looking at the sight from afar off. And when the people of the Jews came to the door of the house, behold, suddenly a power of fire coming forth from within, by means of an angel, burnt up a great multitude of the Jews. And there was great fear throughout all the city; and they glorified God, who had been born of her. And when the procurator saw what had come to pass, he cried out to all the people, saying: Truly he who was born of the virgin, whom you have thought of driving away, is the Son of God; for these signs are those of the true God. And there was a division among the Jews; and many believed in the name of our Lord Jesus Christ, in consequence of the signs that had come to pass.

And after all these wonderful things had come to pass through the mother of God, and ever-virgin Mary the mother of the Lord, while we the apostles were with her in Jerusalem, the Holy Spirit said to us: You know that on the Lord's day the good news was brought to the Virgin Mary by the archangel Gabriel; and on the Lord's day the Savior was born in Bethlehem; and on the Lord's day the children of Jerusalem came forth with palm branches to meet him, saying, Hosanna in the highest, blessed is He that cometh in the name of the Lord; and on the Lord's day He rose from the dead; and on the Lord's day He will come to judge the living and the dead; and on the Lord's day He will come out of heaven, to the glory and honor of the departure of the holy glorious virgin who brought Him forth. And on the same Lord's day the mother of the

Lord says to the apostles: Cast incense, because Christ is coming with a host of angels; and, behold, Christ is at hand, sitting on a throne of cherubim. And while we were all praying, there appeared innumerable multitudes of angels, and the Lord mounted upon cherubim in great power; and, behold, a stream of light coming to the holy virgin, because of the presence of her only-begotten Son, and all the powers of the heavens fell down and adored Him. And the Lord, speaking to His mother, said: Mary. And she answered and said: Here am I, Lord. And the Lord said to her: Grieve not, but let thy heart rejoice and be glad; for thou hast found grace to behold the glory given to me by my Father. And the holy mother of God looked up, and saw in Him a glory which it is impossible for the mouth of man to speak of, or to apprehend. And the Lord remained beside her, saying: Behold, from the present time thy precious body will be transferred to paradise, and thy holy soul to the heavens to the treasures of my Father in exceeding brightness, where there is peace and joy of the holy angels,--and other things besides. And the mother of the Lord answered and said to him: Lay Thy right hand upon me, O Lord, and bless me. And the Lord stretched forth His undefiled right hand, and blessed her. And she laid hold of His undefiled right hand, and kissed it, saying: I adore this right hand, which created the heaven and the earth; and I call upon Thy much to be praised name Christ, O God, the King of the ages, the only-begotten of the Father, to receive Thine handmaid, Thou who didst deign to be brought forth by me, in a low estate, to save the race of men through Thine ineffable dispensation; do Thou bestow Thine aid upon every man calling upon, or praying to, or naming the the name of, Thine handmaid. And while she is saying this, the apostles, having gone up to her feet and adored, say: O mother of the Lord, leave a blessing to the world, since thou art going away from it. For thou hast blessed it, and raised it up when it was ruined, by bringing forth the Light of the world. And the mother of the Lord prayed, and in her prayer spoke thus: O God, who through Thy great goodness hast sent from the heavens Thine only-begotten Son to dwell in my humble body, who hast deigned to be born of me, humble as I am, have mercy upon the world, and every soul that calls upon Thy name. And again she prayed, and said: O Lord, King of the heavens, Son of the living God, accept every man who calls upon Thy name, that Thy birth may be glorified. And again she prayed, and said: O Lord Jesus Christ, who art all-powerful in heaven and on earth, in this appeal I implore Thy holy name; in every time and place where there is made mention of my name, make that place holy, and glorify those that glorify Thee through my name, accepting of such persons all their offering, and all their supplication, and all their prayer. And when she had thus prayed, the Lord said to His mother: Let thy heart rejoice and be glad; for every favour and every gift has been given to thee from my Father in heaven, and from me, and from the Holy Spirit: every soul that calls upon thy name shall not be ashamed, but shall find mercy, and comfort, and support, and confidence, both in the world that now is, and in that which is to come, in the presence of my Father in the heavens.

And the Lord turned and said to Peter: The time has come to begin the singing of the hymn. And Peter having begun the singing of the hymn, all the powers of the heavens responded with the Alleluiah. And then the face of the mother of the Lord shone brighter than the light, and she rose up and blessed each of the apostles with her own hand, and all gave glory to God; and the Lord stretched forth His undefiled hands, and received her holy and blameless soul. And with the departure of her blameless soul the place was filled with perfume and ineffable light; and, behold, a voice out of the heaven was heard, saying: Blessed art thou among women. And Peter, and I John, and Paul, and Thomas, ran and wrapped up her precious feet for the consecration; and the twelve apostles put her precious and holy body upon a couch, and carried it. And, behold, while they were carrying her, a certain well-born Hebrew, Jephonias by name, running against the body, put his hands upon the couch; and, behold, an angel of the Lord by invisible power, with a sword of fire, cut off his two hands from his shoulders, and made them hang about the couch, lifted up in the air. And at this miracle which had come to pass all the people of the Jews who beheld it cried out: Verily, He that was brought forth by thee is the true God, O mother of God, ever-virgin Mary. And Jephonias himself, when Peter ordered him, that the wonderful things of God might be showed forth, stood up behind the couch, and cried out: Holy Mary, who broughtest forth Christ who is God, have mercy upon me. And Peter turned and said to him: In the name of Him who was born of her, thy hands which have been taken away from thee, will be fixed on again. And immediately, at the word of Peter, the hands hanging by the couch of the Lady came, and were fixed on Jephonias. And he believed, and glorified Christ, God who had been born of her.

And when this miracle had been done, the apostles carried the couch, and laid down her precious and holy body in Gethsemane in a new tomb. And, behold, a perfume of sweet savor came forth out of the holy sepulchre of our Lady the mother of God; and for three days the voices of invisible angels were heard glorifying Christ our God, who had been born of her. And when the third day was ended, the voices were no longer heard; and from that time forth all knew that her spotless and precious body had been transferred to paradise.

And after it had been transferred, behold, we see Elisabeth the mother of St. John the Baptist, and Anna the mother of the Lady, and Abraham, and Isaac, and Jacob, and David, singing the Alleluiah, and all the choirs of the saints adoring the holy relics of the mother of the Lord, and the place full of light, than which light nothing could be more brilliant, and an abundance of perfume in that place to which her precious and holy body had been transferred in paradise, and the melody of those praising Him who had been born of her--sweet melody, of which there is no satiety, such as is given to virgins, and them only, to hear. We apostles, therefore, having beheld the sudden precious translation of her holy body, glorified God, who had shown us His wonders at the departure of the mother of our Lord Jesus Christ, whose prayers and good offices may we all be deemed worthy to receive. under her shelter, and support, and protection, both in the world that now is and in that which is to come, glorifying in every time and place her only-begotten Son, along with the Father and the Holy Spirit, for ever and ever. Amen.

<u>Conclusion</u>

I hope this book has richly blessed all who reads its. These historical documents referred to as the Christian writing, I hope will help all that reader them have a better understanding of the Bible and Event that took place so long a go.

If you are born again Christian may our lord and savior open your mind and heart to help you grow in the grace of his word.

If you are reading this book and by chance you do not know the lord as your personal savoir. Let me take this opportunity to invite you to open your heart to Jesus. And accept the free gift Jesus offers to you. Does

not matter who you or where you are you, you do not have to be in the church or talking to a minister, all you have to do is ask him to forgive your sins and ask him into your heart and then try and live the best life you can. You read the Bible to learn to life a more fruitful and happy life.
Knowing that when the day comes to leave this earth, leave the shell we call the body. You will be welcomed into a new home call Heaven. We see many of the people we went to school with or people we have worked with die and leave this earth.
It's a date we all have sometime in our future. My pray is you will be there.

One of the best verses in all the bible is John 3: 16
John chapter 3 of the bible verses 16-20

16   For God so loved the world that he gave his only begotten Son, that whosoever believeth in him should not perish, but have everlasting life.
17   For God sent not his Son into the world to condemn the world; but that the world through him might be saved.
18   He that believeth on him is not condemned: but he that believeth not is

condemned already, because he hath not believed in the name of the only begotten Son of God.

19   And this is the condemnation, that light is come into the world, and men loved darkness rather than light, because their deeds were evil.

20   For every one that doeth evil hateth the light, neither cometh to the light, lest his deeds should be reproved.

You hear people say they are born a gain, what this means is they started a new life living the best they can for our Lord and following his examples He has given us in the Bible.

There are two books in Heaven one is call the book of life. If you ask the Lord to save you and believe in him, your name is then written into the book of life. And likewise erased out of the book of Death, every one born on this earth on the day they become aware of right and wrong there name is entered into the book of Death. Let me try and put it in another way the book of life is all the people that belongs to our Lord and Savor Jesus Christ. The book of Death is all the people that belong to Satan the Devil, the old snake that rules over the earth.

Revelation 20:15

And whosoever was not found written in the book of life was cast into the lake of fire.

Genesis 6:3

And the LORD said, My spirit shall not always strive with man

The gift of life is free for the asking, it cost you nothing. Ask and believe and it's yours. But do not put it off thinking you can use it later on, it can be a limited time offer for them who think the can use it just before they die.

How do I ask for this free gift of love?

Dear God I acknowledge I have sin, born into a world of sin,
And deserve the judgment. I ask for your mercy and grant me your free gift. The gift of life everlasting, I now receive you into my heart as my Lord and my Savior.
Thank you Lord for taking my place in Death, Knowing this is the reason you came

to earth and Died on the cross, that in your Love I may live. I will now turn away from my sins and will live the best I can to please you my Lord. Knowing that being human I will fall short at times.
But I will seek your forgiveness know that you love for me is everlasting.
Save me Lord Jesus Amen

May Our Lord Jesus Christ be with you and bless you all.

Rev Danny Davis

Reno_27320@yahoo.com

Made in the USA
Columbia, SC
28 April 2023

15906659R00043